BABY BOOMER
TRIVIA

Beth Jones

BOK2018

RIVER OAK
PUBLISHING

Baby Boomer Trivia
Copyright © 2002 by Beth Ann Jones
This edition published in 2002 by RiverOak Publishing
exclusively for Hallmark Cards, Inc.
1-58919-940-5

www.hallmark.com

DEDICATION

This book is dedicated to

Waverly High School

Class of 1977

Lansing, Michigan

INTRODUCTION

I wanted to marry Donny Osmond! I wanted to be Marcia Brady. I waited day after day for Gilligan, the Skipper, too, the millionaire and his wife, the movie star, the professor, and Mary Ann to find a way to get off that island! I loved my Archie lunch box, bell bottoms, patchouli incense, hanging macramé plant holders, and The Carpenters on 8-track! I still know all the words to "I Think I Love You!"

I am a Baby Boomer, born in 1959, and this was my culture! If you were born between 1946 and 1964, then we have a lot in common. We have our own history, our own code words, our own memories—all seventy-six million of us! We grew up in a time of unprecedented history—the 60s and the 70s. Our "group" changed the diaper industry, and the lunch-box business. We put Coca-Cola and McDonald's on the map! Now we are in our 30s, 40s, and 50s! We're busy dads and soccer moms. Our old clothes are now cool again! We're driving mini-vans and sport utility vehicles. We're sending e-mail, talking on cellular phones, and surfing the web. We're on treadmills and in step-aerobic classes by the hordes, and a few of us are even getting serious about anti-wrinkle creams. We are the envied generation, and we must never forget the things that made growing up as a Baby Boomer so fun!

Take a sentimental journey through this little quiz book and prove, to whoever cares, you really did wear bell bottoms—the first time they were popular!

Beth Jones

How To Use This Book

Who are you? A "Die-Hard Baby Boomer" or a "Baby Boomer Wanna-Be"? Take the "Little Quiz" and find out! We've listed 142 questions that cover numerous areas of our lives as Baby Boomers. From old TV shows to fashion, fads, movies, and music—we tried to include a few questions from every area we could think of.

1. **Have Fun:** Get a pencil and take the "Little Quiz" yourself by filling in the blanks and following the prompts. The correct answers are in the back of this book.

2. **Throw a Party:** Host a "Boomer" party and rent *The Brady Bunch Movie*, *Mission Impossible*, *Flipper*, or any of the other remake movies we made famous—and have your whole party take the quiz.

3. **Get a Date or Meet New Friends:** Carry this book with you at all times. Whenever you see someone who looks "babyboomerish," just begin quizzing them! What a great ice breaker!

4. **Become Popular:** Give this book as a gift to all your Baby Boomer friends! It's a great birthday present. Give it to everyone at your next class reunion, and you will be the coolest person ever!

Footnote: This book is not based upon scientific study! Have fun!

Correct answers
begin on page 143.
Add up your score
on page 152
to find out if you really
are a Baby Boomer!

"Bell Bottoms and Hip _____"

NAME THESE TEEN HEARTTHROBS.

Donny   _____

Davey   _____

Bobby   _____

David   _____

THINGS YOUR MOTHER SAID . . .

"Close the door. Were you born in a _____."

"If you think it's my job to pick up after you, _____."

"Eat your food. There are children _____."

"Your room looks like a _____."

"HEY, HEY WE'RE THE

4

How Long was "The Minnow's" tour supposed to be?

NAME GEORGE JETSON'S . . .

Wife _____

Son _____

Daughter _____

Dog _____

WHAT WERE P.F. FLYERS & RED BALL JETS?

"DANGER! DANGER!
GO BACK
WILL ROBINSON!"
WHO SAID THAT?

REMEMBER THESE SLOGANS?

Where did you go if you wanted to "have it your way"?

_____

Whose generation was it? _____

What did you deserve? _____

What did they want to teach the world to do?

_____

9

WHO IS "MRS. BEASLEY"?

REMEMBER THESE FADS?

Hula _____   Lava _____

Platform _____   Pet _____

Mood _____   Pocca _____

CAN YOU WHISTLE THE MY THREE SONS THEME SONG?

GO AHEAD!

IN ONE OF THE POPULAR DR. SEUSS BOOKS, WHO DIDN'T LIKE GREEN EGGS AND HAM?

13

NAME THE ENTIRE BRADY BUNCH.

_____   _____

_____   _____

_____   _____

_____   _____

WHAT "CLASSIC" SONG PLAYED AT THE END OF EVERY HIGH SCHOOL DANCE IN THE '70s?

15

NAME BUFFY AND JODY'S . . .

Uncle _____

Older Sister _____

Caregiver _____

WHAT ARE "COOTIES" AND "COOTIE SPRAY"?

CAN YOU SING THE BEVERLY HILLBILLIES THEME SONG?

GO AHEAD!

WHICH ONE WASN'T A PART OF OUR CHILDHOOD?

_____ Cap'n Crunch

_____ Captain & Tennille

_____ Captain Kangaroo

_____ Captain Nemo

_____ Captain Jean Luc Picard

_____ Captain Kirk

WHAT DOES IT MEAN TO "POP A WHEELIE"?

NAME THE THREE STARS OF THE MOD SQUAD.

_____

_____

_____

WHAT GROUP SANG, "C'MON GET HAPPY" AND "I THINK I LOVE YOU"?

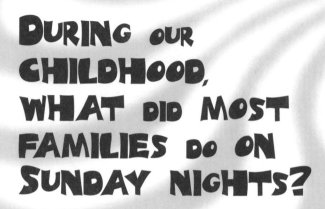

DURING OUR CHILDHOOD, WHAT DID MOST FAMILIES DO ON SUNDAY NIGHTS?

NAME THE CHARACTERS OF *THE DICK VAN DYKE SHOW.*

_____ and _____ Petrie

and their son _____

24

CAN YOU SING THE McDonald's Big Mac Jingle?

Go ahead!

WHO ARE COLONEL MUSTARD, PROFESSOR PLUM, AND MISS SCARLET?

"KAPOW!", "BASH!", "ZAP!" WHAT SHOW?

NAME "THE JACKSON FIVE."

_____   _____

_____   _____

_____

"I SEE SUSIE, I SEE TOMMY, I SEE MICHELLE, AND I SEE YOU, TOO!"

WHAT SHOW?

_____

29

NAME THESE '70s MOVIES.

The luxury ocean liner that sank _____

The high-rise building on fire _____

The shark that kept everyone out of the water

_____

The boxer who wouldn't be defeated_____

WHO ARE WALLY CLEAVER AND EDDIE HASKELL?

WHAT WAS A . . .

Pixie _____

Bee Hive _____

Shag _____

BILLIE JO, BETTY JO, AND BOBBY JO FROM PETTICOAT JUNCTION LIVED IN WHAT TOWN?

_____

REMEMBER THESE SONGS?

What wouldn't spoil a whole bunch of girls?

_____

Who was Jeremiah?

_____

What was the loneliest number?

_____

He wasn't heavy, what was he?

_____

HOW DO YOU "TIE-DYE" A T-SHIRT?

What did it mean if your parents had to call you by your first, middle, and last name?

Can you describe "the look"? Mother's glare?

Can you remember "the" sound? Dad's snap?

CAN YOU HUM THE BONANZA THEME SONG?

GO AHEAD!

"AND THAT'S THE WAY IT IS. . . ." WHO SAID THIS EVERY EVENING AT 6:00 P.M.?

Can you say
"Peace and Love" in "pig Latin"?

Go ahead!

Did you know "jibberish,"
a great code language
parents didn't understand?

Let's hear it!

REMEMBER THE WILD KINGDOM?

Who was the host? _____

Who was his assistant? _____
(Hint: "Watch now as he wrestles the wild alligator.")

Who was the *major* sponsor? _____

40

IN THE '70s, WHO WERE THE TWO STARS IN THE HIT MOVIE GREASE?

WHAT REALLY "COOL" THING DID WE DO TO OUR BIKES WITH A DECK OF CARDS AND CLOTHESPINS?

WHO ARE OPIE AND AUNT BEE?

WHAT TOWN DID THEY LIVE IN?

Name everyone in the Partridge Family.

_____   _____

_____   _____

_____   _____

NAME THESE GROUPS.

"Jefferson_____"

"Three Dog _____"

"The Moody_____"

"Creedence _____"

45

CAN YOU SING THE GILLIGAN'S ISLAND THEME SONG?

GO AHEAD?

NAME JOHNNY QUEST'S . . .

Best Friend _____

Dog _____

REMEMBER THESE CARS?

If you were driving in your car and saw a "Volkswagen Bug,"
what did you say and do to the person sitting next to you?

_____

Which car was not part of our era?

_____ Gremlin   _____ Pacer   _____ Pinto
_____ Mini-Van   _____ Matchbox   _____ Chitty-Chitty
                                                          Bang-Bang

ON GREEN ACRES . . .

Who drove the junk truck?

_____

What was the pig's name?

_____

NAME THESE POPULAR GROUPS FROM THE 60s.

They sang "Help Me Rhonda":

_____

They sang "Surf City":

_____

They sang "Blowin' in the Wind":

_____

Their "Sold Out" album was a Billboard bestseller:

_____

WHAT DID THURSTON HOWELL CALL MRS. HOWELL?

DID YOU PLAY THESE OUTDOOR GAMES?

"Kick the _____"

"Einey-iney _____"

"Mother_____"

"Red Rover _____"

"Capture the_____"

"Dodge _____"

WHAT CHARACTER SAID, "GOLLY"?

(HINT: PRONOUNCED - "GAWAWLLY.")

WHAT ARE. . .

Teaberry, Black Jack, Clove, and Beeman's?

_____

Black Cow Sucker _____

Zots _____

WHO ARE COLONEL KLINK AND SCHULTZ?

IN THE GAME MONOPOLY®, WHAT COLOR ARE ST. JAMES PLACE, TENNESSEE AVENUE, AND NEW YORK AVENUE?

?

CAN YOU WHISTLE THE ANDY GRIFFITH SHOW THEME SONG?

DO IT!

REMEMBER YOUR METALLIC PURPLE "STINGRAY"?

WHAT WERE "BANANA SEATS" AND "SISSY BARS"?

NAME THE THREE BOYS ON MY THREE SONS.

_____

_____

_____

60

WHAT FEMALE VOCALISTS SANG THESE SONGS?

"Stop In the Name of Love" _____

"I Am Woman, Hear Me Roar" _____

"I Feel the Earth Move" _____

"Killing Me Softly" _____

WHAT WAS UNVEILED AT THE NEW YORK WORLD'S FAIR ON APRIL 17, 1964?

IT COST ONLY $2,368 AND COULD ACCOMMODATE A FAMILY OF FOUR!

HOW MUCH WERE THE CLAMPETTS REALLY WORTH?

WHAT DID JETHRO BODINE CALL A SWIMMING POOL?

NAME POPEYE'S . . .

Girlfriend _____

Arch Rival _____

WHAT DID THESE CHARACTERS WANT?

The Tin Man _____

The Scarecrow _____

The Lion _____

Dorothy _____

WHERE WERE YOU ON NOVEMBER 22, 1963?

CAN YOU NAME . . .

The highest-rated police show in TV history?

_____

The highest-rated, longest-running lawyer show in TV history?

_____

WHAT DO THE WORDS "SHAG" AND "OLIVE GREEN" MEAN TO YOU?

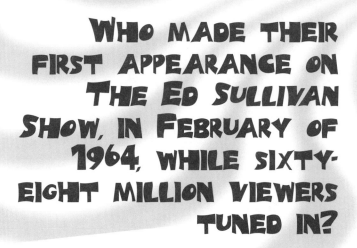

WHO MADE THEIR FIRST APPEARANCE ON **THE ED SULLIVAN SHOW**, IN FEBRUARY OF 1964, WHILE SIXTY-EIGHT MILLION VIEWERS TUNED IN?

WHO SANG THESE SONGS?

"Takin' Care of Business"

_____

"Takin' It to the Streets"

_____

REMEMBER THESE COMMERCIALS?

"Shake and Bake and I _____"

Everyone would be in love with you if you were what kind of hot dog?

_____

What did the "Frito-Bandito" love? _____

What did astronauts drink? _____

"When I was your _____,

I walked five _____

    to school in six feet of

_____,

    bare _____,

    up _____,

    both _____."

72

WHAT IS THE NAME OF THE BEST-SELLING FLEETWOOD MAC ALBUM?

"SMILE, YOU'RE ON

"_____"

WHICH TV SHOW BEST DESCRIBES THE FAMILY YOU GREW UP IN?

_____ *The Munsters*

_____ *The Little Rascals*

_____ *The Twilight Zone*

_____ *The Three Stooges*

_____ None of the Above

_____ All of the Above

POPULAR DANCE IN THE '70S.

"FUNKY

_____ "

"SOCK IT TO ME, SOCK IT TO ME, SOCK IT TO ME!" WHAT SHOW?

WHO'S HERBIE?

Name these TV Game Shows:

"My Name Is . . ." _____

"Circle Gets the Square." _____

"Bachelor Number One." _____

"Would You Sign In, Please?" _____

WHAT TWO CIRCULAR SYMBOLS WERE POPULAR IN OUR ERA?

DRAW THEM!

NAME THESE SINGERS/BANDS:

"Engelbert _____."

"Herb Alpert and the _____."

"Paul Revere and the _____."

"Herman's _____."

CAN YOU SING YOUR HIGH SCHOOL FIGHT SONG? GO AHEAD!

REMEMBER THESE TV SHOWS?

What is "black gold" and "Texas tea"? _____

Who had "hair of gold" like their mother? _____

What kind of "time" did the Flintstones have? _____

Why was the "tiny ship" tossed? _____

WHO SAID, "WE'RE GOING TO HAVE A REALLY BIG SHOE!"

NAME THE POPULAR MEN'S SUIT OF THE '70s.

"POLYESTER   "

WHO WERE THE TWO BOYS ON FLIPPER?

WHAT WAS THE NAME OF THE POPULAR DORIS DAY SONG?

WHAT DID THE WHAM-O CORPORATION FIRST PRODUCE IN 1958?

REMEMBER THIS TV SHOW?

Who were Agent 86 and Agent 99? _____

What did Agent 86 have in his shoe? _____

How did each episode of this show begin? _____

"ONE SMALL STEP FOR MAN, ONE GIANT LEAP FOR MANKIND."

WHO SAID THAT?

"BOOK 'EM, DAN-O!" WHAT SHOW?

NAME THESE POPULAR MALE VOCALISTS:

Loggins & _____

Cat _____

Harry _____

Elton _____

WHAT WAS "TIGER BEAT"?

WHO SAID, "BEEP, BEEP"?

NAME THE LONE RANGER'S . . .

Horse _____

Best Friend _____

CAN YOU SING THE BRADY BUNCH THEME SONG?
GO AHEAD!

WHAT DID MR. WHIPPLE TELL US NOT TO SQUEEZE?

_____ Mrs. Whipple

_____ The Charmin

_____ The Toothpaste

NAME THE THREE ORIGINAL "CHARLIE'S ANGELS."

_____

_____

_____

98

WHAT DID JIM CROCE WANT TO SAVE IN A BOTTLE?

IN THE '60s, THOUSANDS OF PEOPLE HAD A SPIRITUAL AWAKENING. WHAT WAS IT CALLED?

_____ Movement

How did every episode of these TV shows end?

The Carol Burnett Show _____

The Waltons _____

REMEMBER THESE CLASSICS?

What did Mary Poppins say a spoon full of sugar would do?

_____

Who was the piano player on *Charlie Brown*? _____

Who would dream in her own little corner, in her own little room?

_____

What was the name of Dorothy's dog? _____

How Many of These Interior Fashion Trends did You Grow Up With?

_____ Hanging Macramé Plant Holder

_____ Beaded Room Divider

_____ Red, Orange, or Harvest Gold Counter Tops

_____ Foil-like Wallpaper

WHO WERE ROSEANNE ROSEANNADANNA AND EMILY LATTILLA?

WHO SANG THESE SONGS, "GO AWAY LITTLE GIRL," "SWEET AND INNOCENT," AND "YO-YO"?

WHO WERE JAMES T. WEST AND ARTEMUS GORDON?

WHAT WOULD "SELF-DESTRUCT" IN FIVE SECONDS?

THINGS YOUR DAD SAID . . .

"How would you like a
_____ sandwich?"

"You're cruisin'
_____."

"Do you want me to stop this car and
_____?"

108

NAME THESE POPULAR MALE AND FEMALE VOCALISTS . . .

Who sang "When Will I Be Loved?" and "That'll Be the Day?"

Who sang "You've Got a Friend" and "Fire and Rain"?

REMEMBER THE DRIVE-IN MOVIE THEATER?

What happened if you tried to enter at the exit?

_____

How many people could fit in your trunk?

_____

WHO WAS ARCHIE'S GIRLFRIEND?

_____ Betty

_____ Veronica

WHO SANG THESE SONGS?

"Stayin' Alive" _____

"Up, Up, and Away" _____

"Knock Three Times" _____

NAME THESE CARTOONS.

Mighty _____.

Under _____.

Scooby _____.

Lippy the Lion and _____.

George of _____.

THESE CHARACTERS WERE ON WHAT TV SHOWS?

Adam, Hoss, and Little Joe _____

Festus and Miss Kitty _____

MR. SPOCK OF STAR TREK FAME WAS . . .

Part human and part _____.

WHO WAS THE STAR OF THAT GIRL?

REMEMBER THESE FOOD AND DRINK ITEMS?

Space Food _____

Bonomo Turkish _____

_____ Crush

DESCRIBE THE CLASSIC SATURDAY NIGHT FEVER DISCO OUTFIT.
DID YOU HAVE ONE?

Fabric _____

Color _____

Lapels _____

WHO SANG THESE SONGS?

"Close to You" _____

"Feelings" _____

"Saturday, in the Park" _____

FINISH THESE TV SHOW TITLES:

Man From _____

I Dream _____

The Bionic_____

WHAT USED TO BE INCLUDED IN THE TRADING CARD PACKAGES?

(HINT: BASEBALL CARDS, BATMAN CARDS, BEATLES CARDS, ETC.)

REMEMBER THESE CHARACTERS?

Bullwinkle and _____

Yogi Bear and _____

Gumby and _____

Tom Terrific and His Mighty Dog _____

"THE SOUNDS OF SILENCE" AND "BRIDGE OVER TROUBLED WATER"

WHO SANG THESE?

WHAT THREE ASSASSINATIONS took PLACE IN OUR CHILDHOOD?

_____

_____

_____

WHO ARE MONTY HALL AND CAROL MERRILL?

WHEN WE WERE KIDS, WHAT KIND OF CANDY COULD WE BUY FOR A PENNY?

WHO SAID, "MY NAME IS EDITH ANN, AND I AM FIVE YEARS OLD."?

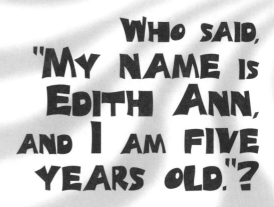

WHAT WAS THE VAN OF CHOICE IN OUR CHILDHOOD?

WHAT WAS "WOODSTOCK"?

_____ A bird in the _Peanuts_ cartoon.

_____ A gathering of thousands of hippies for a huge rock concert in Bethel, New York in August of 1969.

_____ Both of the above

WHICH WORD DESCRIBES YOUR TEEN YEARS?

_____ Groovy

_____ Peace

_____ Love

_____ Cool

_____ Bogue

_____ Heavy

_____ Bomb

_____ Hip

NAME THESE TV SHOWS.

Welcome Back _____

McHale's _____

Please Don't Eat _____

The Six Million _____

ACCORDING TO THE
TV SHOW THEME
SONG, WHAT KIND
OF MAN WAS
DANIEL BOONE?

"Flower _____"

Do you remember what those little flower decals were called?

NAME AT LEAST TWO BARBRA STREISAND MOVIES YOU SAW AS A KID.

?

_____

_____

NAME TWO DETECTIVE TV SHOWS FROM OUR ERA.

_____

_____

WHO SANG, "I GOT YOU BABE"?

WHO WERE THE "HONEYMOONERS"? NAME THEM.

_____   _____

_____   _____

PERFUMES OF OUR ERA, CACHET, AMBUSH . . .

Wind _____

Jean _____

Old _____

WHO WAS LITTLE RICKY?

Remember the "Name Game" song?

Can you sing it with your name?

(Hint: "Debbie, Debbie . . ." or "Steve, Steve . . ." or your name!)

MORE THINGS YOUR MOTHER SAID:

"Do you think I don't have anything else to do but
_____?"

You said, "Tommy's mom said he could. . . ."
Your mom said, "Well, I'm
_____!"

You said, "Mom, everyone's doing it."
Your mom said, "If everyone jumped
_____!"

You asked, "Mom, why do I have to do that . . . ?" or "Why can't I do that . . . ?"
Your mom said, "Because I
_____!"

FINALLY, REMEMBER THIS MATCHMAKING SCENARIO?

You are the "messenger" and you say, "Johnny, do you like Michelle?" He replies, "Does she like me?" You say, "If you like her, she likes you." He responds by buying Michelle an "ID bracelet" and asking her if she wants to "go steady." They never have another conversation, and technically, twenty-five years later, they are still "going together." What grade were you in when this scene took place?

CORRECT ANSWERS

Put an "X" in the blank space if you got all or part of a multiple-choice question correct!

1. _____ Bell Bottoms and Hip Huggers! (Remember Elephant & Whale Bells? How about homemade "rip the side seam & insert the fabric" bells ... and we thought those were so cool!)

2. _____ Donny Osmond; Davey Jones; Bobby Sherman; David Cassidy

3. _____ "Close the door; were you born in a barn?"; "If you think it's my job to pick up after you, you've got another thing coming!"; "Eat your food. There are children starving in India"; "Your room looks like a pigsty!" or "Your room looks like a tornado hit it!" (Universal sayings ... where do mother's get these? How many of these have you said?)

4. _____ Monkees

5. _____ A three-hour tour

6. _____ Jane, his wife; boy, Elroy; daughter, Judy; ... and of course, Astro ("Rastro")

7. _____ Tennis Shoes (You could run faster and jump higher, remember?)

8. _____ The robot on *Lost In Space*

9. _____ Burger King; The Pepsi Generation; A Break Today; To Sing

10. _____ Buffy's doll, from the TV show *Family Affair*

11. _____ Hula Hoop; Platform Shoes; Mood Ring; Lava Lamp; Pet Rock; Pocca Beads

12. _____ We trust you! Take the point!
13. _____ Sam I Am (Didn't you love that book? in a nook? with a hook?)
14. _____ Carol, Mike, Marcia, Jan, Cindy, Greg, Peter, Bobby (and of course, Alice!)
15. _____ "Stairway To Heaven"
16. _____ Uncle Bill; Sissy; Mr. French
17. _____ Cooties were germs of the opposite sex, and the spray was invisible protection from those germs! (Remember the "Cootie Catchers" we made by folding a piece of square paper in various ways into four sections?)
18. _____ We trust you! Take the point!
19. _____ Captain Jean Luc Picard (Who?)
20. _____ To ride on the back wheel of a bike, while the front wheel is raised up in the air—the longer the better!
21. _____ Linc; Pete; Julie
22. _____ The Partridge Family
23. _____ We watched *The Wonderful World of Disney!* (On a really special night, we had McDonalds and Jiffy Pop!)
24. _____ Rob and Laura Petrie and their son, Richie
25. _____ We trust you! Take the point!
26. _____ Characters from the game Clue
27. _____ Batman (The Caped Crusader and The Boy Wonder)
28. _____ Michael, Tito, Jermaine, Marlon, and Jackie

29. _____ Romper Room (Did she ever say your name?)
30. _____ *The Poseidon Adventure; The Towering Inferno; Jaws; Rocky*
31. _____ Beaver Cleaver's brother and his best friend ("Hello Mr. and Mrs. Cleaver. Hello Theodore.")
32. _____ A Pixie was a short, little-girls' haircut that we disliked; A Bee Hive was a really tall "mom" hairdo; A Shag was *the* hair cut of the 70s!
33. _____ Hooterville
34. _____ One bad apple; A bullfrog; One is; My brother
35. _____ Put rubber bands all over various "wadded" sections of the t-shirt. Dip the shirt in your favorite color of Rit Dye. Rinse it out. Let it dry and remove all the rubber bands. Voila! (How about your jeans? Did you throw your jeans in a swimming pool to get them to fade?)
36. _____ You were in big trouble! The glare—tight lips, teeth clenched, finger pointed! The snap—loud and scary!
37. _____ We trust you! Take the point!
38. _____ Walter Cronkite
39. _____ "Eace-pay and Ove-lay" Jibberish was where you put a "thg" sound after the first letter of each syllable!
40. _____ Marlin Perkins; Jim; Mutual of Omaha
41. _____ John Travolta; Oliva Newton-John
42. _____ We used clothespins to put baseball cards, or other cards, on our bike near the spokes so they would make that "flutter" sound.

43. ____ Characters on *The Andy Griffith Show*; Mayberry, North Carolina
44. ____ Shirley, Keith, Laurie, Danny, Chris, Tracy (and of course, Mr. Kincaid)
45. ____ Jefferson Airplane or Starship; Three Dog Night; The Moody Blues; Creedence Clearwater Revival
46. ____ We trust you! Take the point!
47. ____ Hadji; Bandit
48. ____ You say, "Slug bug" and you "slug" your neighbor on the arm (Was this just a girl thing?); Mini-van
49. ____ Mr. Haney drove the junk truck; Arnold Ziffel was the famous pig.
50. ____ The Beach Boys; Jan and Dean; Bob Dylan & Peter, Paul, and Mary both sang "Blowin'"; The Kingston Trio
51. ____ Lovey
52. ____ Kick the Can; Einey-iney Over; Mother, May I?; Red Rover, Red Rover; Capture the Flag; Dodge Ball
53. ____ Gomer Pyle
54. ____ Gum; chocolate-covered sucker; fizzy candies
55. ____ Characters from *Hogan's Heroes*
56. ____ Orange
57. ____ *Howdy Doody*
58. ____ We trust you! Take the point!
59. ____ Stingrays were the coolest! Banana seats were the long seats; sissy bars were the tall bars on the back of the seat and were great for popping wheelies!

60. _____ Ernie, Chip, Robby
61. _____ Diana Ross and the Supremes; Helen Reddy; Carole King; Roberta Flack
62. _____ Ford Mustang (Can you believe it?)
63. _____ The Clampetts were worth $25 million; Jethro called a swimming pool a "cement pond."
64. _____ Olive Oyl; Bluto or Brutus
65. _____ Tin Man wanted a heart; Scarecrow wanted brains; Lion wanted courage; Dorothy wanted to go home.
66. _____ That is the day that John F. Kennedy was assassinated.
67. _____ *Dragnet* "The names have been changed to protect the innocent"; *Perry Mason*
68. _____ "Shag" and "olive green" were the style and color of carpet in most every home in America!
69. _____ The Beatles
70. _____ Bachman-Turner Overdrive—also known as BTO; The Doobie Brothers
71. _____ Shake and Bake and I helped!; Oscar Meyer Weiner; Frito's Corn Chips; Tang
72. _____ "When I was your age, I walked five miles to school in six feet of snow, bare foot, up hill, both ways!"
73. _____ Rumours
74. _____ Candid Camera
75. _____ Take the point! (Does this explain why some families are dysfunctional and co-dependent?)
76. _____ Funky Chicken

77. _____ Laugh In
78. _____ The Love Bug
79. _____ *To Tell the Truth; Hollywood Squares; The Dating Game; What's My Line?*
80. _____ A happy face and the peace sign ☺ ☮
81. _____ Engelbert Humperdink; Herb Alpert and the Tijuana Brass; Paul Revere and the Raiders; Herman's Hermits
82. _____ We trust you! Take the point!
83. _____ Oil from *The Beverly Hillbillies*; The very lovely girls on *The Brady Bunch*; A Yabba-Dabba-Do time; The weather started getting rough.
84. _____ Ed Sullivan
85. _____ Polyester leisure suit
86. _____ Bud; Sandy
87. _____ "Que Será, Será"
88. _____ Hoola Hoop
89. _____ Agent 86 (Maxwell Smart) and Agent 99 were characters on *Get Smart*; Maxwell Smart had a phone in his shoe; Each episode opened with them walking through a variety of opening doors.
90. _____ Neil Armstrong
91. _____ *Hawaii Five-O*
92. _____ Loggins & Messina; Cat Stevens; Harry Chapin; Elton John
93. _____ A teen magazine (It had all the scoop and great photos of the teen stars!)
94. _____ The *Road Runner* (How many times did the Coyote die?)

95. _____ Silver; Tonto
96. _____ We trust you! Take the point!
97. _____ The Charmin
98. _____ Farah Fawcett; Kate Jackson; Jaclyn Smith
99. _____ Time
100. _____ The Jesus Movement
101. _____ Carol Burnett pulled on her ear; The Waltons went through a "Goodnight John-Boy" exercise.
102. _____ Sugar makes the medicine go down; Schroeder was the piano player; Cinderella; Toto
103. _____ Take the point! (How many hanging macramé plant holders did you have?)
104. _____ Characters played by Gilda Radner on *Saturday Night Live*
105. _____ Donny Osmond of course!
106. _____ The stars of the *Wild, Wild West*
107. _____ Cassette tape on the beginning of the show *Mission Impossible*
108. _____ "How would you like a knuckle sandwich?"; "You're cruisin' for a bruisin'"; "Do you want me to stop this car and turn around?" or "…give you a spanking?" Take a point!
109. _____ Linda Ronstadt; James Taylor
110. _____ Your tires were popped by the spikes; You didn't sneak people into the movie in your trunk did you?
111. _____ Veronica

112. ____ The Bee Gees; The 5th Dimension; Tony Orlando and Dawn
113. ____ *Mighty Mouse; Underdog; Scooby Doo; Lippy the Lion & Hardy Har-Har; George of the Jungle*
114. ____ *Bonanza; Gunsmoke*
115. ____ Vulcan
116. ____ Marlo Thomas
117. ____ Space Food Sticks; Bonomo's Turkish Taffy; Orange Crush
118. ____ Fabric was polyester; Color was white or powder blue; Lapels were huge
119. ____ The Carpenters; Morris Albert; Chicago
120. ____ *Man From U.N.C.L.E.; I Dream of Jeannie; The Bionic Woman*
121. ____ A piece of gum! (Whatever happened to that piece of gum?)
122. ____ Rocky; Boo-Boo; Pokey; Manfred (Remember this segment on Captain Kangaroo?)
123. ____ Simon and Garfunkel
124. ____ John F. Kennedy; Robert Kennedy; Martin Luther King Jr.
125. ____ The host and assistant of the game show, *Let's Make A Deal*
126. ____ Bit-O-Honey; Bazooka Bubble Gum; Shoestring Licorice; Lipstick; Wax Lips; plus more! Take the point!
127. ____ Lily Tomlin
128. ____ Volkswagen Bus
129. ____ Both
130. ____ Take the point!

131. _____ *Welcome Back, Kotter; McHale's Navy; Please Don't Eat the Daisies; The Six Million Dollar Man*
132. _____ A big man!
133. _____ Flower Power or Flower Child; The flower decals were called "Rickie Tickie Stickies"
134. _____ *The Way We Were; A Star Is Born; Funny Girl; What's Up Doc?*—think of others? Take the point.
135. _____ *Dragnet; Mannix; Columbo; Ironside; The Mod Squad* and others—Take the point!
136. _____ Sonny and Cher
137. _____ Ralph, Alice, Ed, and Trixie
138. _____ Windsong; Jean Naté; Old Spice
139. _____ Lucy and Desi's son on *I Love Lucy*
140. _____ We trust you! Take the point!
141. _____ "Do you think I don't have anything else to do but pick up after you?"; "Well, I'm not Tommy's mom!"; "If everyone jumped off a bridge, would you do it?"; "Because I said so!"
142. _____ 7th grade! It was a junior high thing!

Each Question Is Worth One Point.

Remember this is not Master's Degree stuff! If you got at least half of a multiple question correct, take the point.

TOTAL NUMBER CORRECT:_____

SCORING:

SCORE: 0-50–"Baby-Boomer Wanna-Be"
Okay, who are you and what do you want?
Nice try! Good luck in the search to find your people!

SCORE: 51-100–"Might-Know-a-Boomer"
Nice try! But were you really there? We suspect you've
heard stories from true Boomers and wish you'd been there!

SCORE: 101-141–"Big-Time, True-Blue, Die-Hard Baby Boomer"
Congratulations! You are one of us! You really did wear original bell bottoms!

SCORE: 142–"Mother of All Baby Boomers"
Why didn't you write the book?!

ABOUT THE AUTHOR

Beth Jones is a true-blue, die-hard Baby Boomer. From the thrills of the annual "school shopping trip" (to pick out clothes and a new lunchbox), to dancing in go-go boots and hanging out with friends, she thoroughly enjoyed growing up in the '60s and '70s.

Beth graduated from Boston University in 1981, attended Bible School, and now spends most of her spare time in ministry, helping people experience God's best in their lives through one-on-one meetings, public speaking, and writing. She also helps her husband pastor a church and dedicates her time to creating wonderful childhood memories for their four children.

In addition to this "for-fun" book, she has written a series of books designed for Christian growth—*Getting a Grip on the Basics*, *Getting a Grip on Health*, and *Getting a Grip on Prosperous Living*—all published by Harrison House Publishers in Tulsa, Oklahoma.